Char-Griller Charcoal Grill Cookbook for Beginners

The Everything Guide of Charcoal Grill and Smoker Recipe Book for Anyone at Any Occasion

By Danny W. Green

Table of Contents

Description

Create great-tasting food and lifelong memories with Char-Griller!
Amongst the numerous grills available, Char-Griller sets a record. It has gradually become a family-favorite for preparing beef, bacon, and chicken. The Char-griller does not just prepare regular meals; it delivers enchanting delicacies, beautiful memories, and smooth operation. Trust a Char-Griller to do the best job. Professionalism meets capability in the bevy of grills available in the Char-Griller line.   The grills were manufactured with finesse and are capable of extraordinary feats when preparing meals for festivities and celebrations. They are also always ready to perform when dragged along for an outdoor picnic.

This *Char-Griller Cookbook* is a book of tips and tricks for creating magic with your grill. It contains jaw-dropping recipes, a comprehensive guide on how the appliance works, and other nitty-gritty on the equipment. It includes:

> ➢ A Brief History of the Char-Griller
> ➢ Components of the Char-Griller and their Functions
> ➢ Various Models of the Char-Griller
> ➢ Necessary Precautions for the Char-Griller
> ➢ Step-by-Step Operation of the Char-Griller
> ➢ Tips and tricks for grilling with the Char-Griller
> ➢ Common FAQs associated with the Char-Griller
> ➢ **70 sumptuous recipes perfect for Char-Griller.**

Get your copy! Gain access to meals that taste like Paradise.

Introduction

This is the season to grill for fun and have adventures!
Char-Griller maintains its status as one of the most durable and effective grillers. It is considered perfect for all your barbecue needs. The Char-Griller turns every hangout or picnic to a memorable *barbecuing experience.*
Chapter One contains basic information on the history and properties of a Char-griller. Chapters Two and Three covers the tips and tricks of using a Char-griller, and some frequently asked questions. The rest of the book includes mouthwatering recipes that you can try on the Char-griller.
Enjoy!

Chapter 1: Char-Griller 101

What is Char-Griller?

Char-Griller is a collection of affordable, durable, and trust-worthy grills made from heavy-duty steel. They all have two rolling wheels for smooth movement and a large cooking area despite their small size. The Char-Griller chain has evolved from being a modest charcoal kamado grill to boasting of several varieties of grills with different power sources.

Char-Griller can either use charcoal or gas as fuel; it depends on the model purchased. The appliance was built to last; therefore, with proper maintenance, it can last for decades. All the models of the Char-Griller have a dump ash pan for easy cleaning, and a temperature regulator/gauge to monitor meals.

A Brief History of Char-Griller

Char-Griller is a company owned by the Georgias. In the formative years, the company started its outdoor grilling chain with a unique charcoal grill that was designed to produce only the finest barbecue imaginable.

Over the years, Char-Griller improved on the original grill model and has now produced several types of grills to suit different needs. Each grill was meticulously designed and is quite capable of achieving the exceptional meals that were synonymous with the original model. Not long ago, they developed a charcoal grill with a 3-burner propane gas grill known as the kamado cooker. This innovative cooking appliance further emphasized Char-Griller's attention to quality.

Amidst fierce competition, Char-Griller continues to produce durable charcoal grills and smokers at a budget price. Their grills make every cooking experience pleasant and memorable.

Components of the Char-Griller

All models of the Char-Griller are portable and easy to use. Here are some of the components responsible for their functions:

> **Cooking surface:** The Char-Griller doesn't have much in terms of cooking space, but do not be deceived, a lot can be done with it. The small cooking area can prepare enough food for a family of four.

> **Grates:** The grates of the Char-Griller are made from cast-iron to improve their durability and effectiveness when compared to stainless steel. However, cleaning the grates can be tedious as it requires a lot of scrubbing. To have the best use, ensure to clean it after every use.

> **Storage:** Char-Griller has a storage space on one side of the grill for storing cooking materials. Though it may be small, it will hold all you need.

> **Handle:** The scald resistant handle of the Char-Griller is a great safety

feature. The handle allows you to hold the appliance during grilling and after without getting burned.

> **Vent:** The Char-Griller has a large vent on each side to help control the smoke and temperature of the cooking chamber. Some models of the grill have more than two vents, which allows for more precise temperature control.

> **Charcoal drawer:** While the grill has a storage rack on one side, it also has a small drawer for charcoal. And just below the grill is a wire rack that can store briquettes.

> **Lid:** The is the dome-shaped covering that gives the grill an egg shape; the component is necessary for the grill to heat up fast and cook properly. The Char-Griller has a latch on the lid that makes it safe to carry around without opening.

> **Dampers:** The Char-Griller has a damper that regulates the airflow and ensures precise temperature control. A trick to achieve temperatures around 200°F is to close the top and bottom dampers until they are about ¾ closed.

Various Models of the Char-Griller

The manufacturer's desire to produce a grill that is competent and budget-friendly is the inspiration behind every Char-Griller. The Char-Griller manufacturers have grouped their grills into six categories. They include:

> Traditional/Charcoal grills with 23 products
> Dual fuel grills with 7 products
> Kamado grills with 10 products
> Gas grills with 6 products
> Pellet grills with 1 product
> Tailgating with 7 products

In total, there are more than 50 models of Char-Griller grills currently available.

Necessary Precautions for the Char-Griller?

To truly enjoy a Char-Griller, it is best to understand how it works, and this begins with the knowledge of a few precautions. They include:

➢ Never transport the appliance while it is in use.
➢ Never try to use the flame to check for gas leaks
➢ Always keep the grill away from flammable materials
➢ This grill is only for outdoor use
➢ Ensure to keep your hands, face, and body safe from flare-ups, especially when you are opening the lids
➢ Ensure to wear oven mitts or gloves to protect your hands from burns
➢ To suffocate the flame, close the lid and all the dampers. Always ensure to turn off the gas burners and maintain a distance from the grill until the fire is out.
➢ Use water-soaked wood chips for charcoal grills to add a smoky flavor to your food
➢ If you are cooking at a low temperature, always ensure that the lid is closed
➢ Clear up used charcoal after every grilling. If they remain in the grill for too long, it could cause rust.
➢ Grease the trays after every use

- Always preheat the grill for 30 minutes before cooking
- After using the grill, always coat the metal with vegetable oil to prevent rust.
- Never use spirit or petrol when lighting or relighting.

How to Operate the Char-Griller

The operation of any model of the char-griller isn't challenging for both first-timers and seasoned users, however, a simple guide will not hurt anyone. This is a step-by-step instruction on how to operate the kamado char-griller:

1. Before grilling, coat the grill (the barrel and cooking grates) with vegetable oil to protect the coating. However, keep the oil away from hot coals, flame, or fire.
2. Build a medium-sized fire on the fire grate, then stack 2 lbs of charcoal and saturate with lighter fluid. Never use gasoline for this purpose.
3. Open the vents to allow the passage of air.
4. During seasoning, maintain a temperature of 250°F for at least two hours. You can also control the heat with the dampers and adjustable fire grate.
5. Preheat the Char-griller for 15 minutes before cooking your meal.
6. Arrange your meal on the grates and close the Grill lid.
7. Remove the finished meal from the grill and turn it off with dampers or by closing the vents and sealing the cooker.
8. Allow the Char-Griller to cool down before cleaning, drying, and returning to storage.

Chapter 2: Tips and Tricks for Successful grilling with Char-Grillers

Grilling is made easy when you know the right maneuvers to pull at the right time. Here is a list of such tricks to simplify Char-Grilling;

> **Always monitor the temperature**

While grilling, monitor the cooking temperature by adjusting the air vents at the top and bottom of the grill. You can slowly cook ribs at 110◦ C for at least four hours, and if you are baking, you can allow it to cook at 250◦C for 20 minutes. With the charcoal Char-Griller, adjust the temperature by maneuvering the charcoal.

> **Use a meat thermometer**

Don't entirely rely on the cooking time of all the recipes. Always use a meat thermometer to measure the internal temperature of foods.

> **Flavour is a big deal**

When grilling, ensure the meat is slowly cooked and given time to absorb all the smoky flavor. The flavor is what provides the meat with its uniqueness. Professional chefs consider the Char-Griller charcoal grill as the best for a barbecue because of the unique smoky and grilled taste infused into the meat. Use lump charcoal to get the best out of Char-grilling; it emits a more robust flavor that penetrates the meat favorably.

> **Choose the right wood**

The same gentle care used when determining the meat to grill should be employed when choosing the wood to use. Your choice greatly determines the outcome of your barbecue. Using green or fresh wood will only produce an unpleasant smoke that will burn out before cooking starts. Hence, choose only dry and cured wood in smaller chunks; this will give you control over the fire and temperature.

> **Spray your meat for great taste**

The goal is to get a barbecue with a perfect taste and texture. While grilling, keep a spray bottle containing oil, soda, juice, and whiskey. Spray your meat occasionally to preserve moisture on the surface of the meat. Always keep some juice handy when grilling.

> **Trust the process**

Grilling, roasting, and especially smoking, take a lot of time. Exercise patience and trust the Char-Griller to do its job. Rather than stressing over the food while cooking, you can redirect the restless energy to watching the color of the smoke released from the grill. If it is bluish grey, it means the airflow is circulating, and the grill is at the perfect temperature.

Chapter 3: Common FAQs for the Char-Griller

Most beginners and novices have at least one burning question about the char-griller. Here is a list of some of the more common questions asked:

➤ **How do I clean the interior and exterior of the grill?**
Remove sticky food items from the grates of the Char-Griller by scrubbing it with a grill brush. After this is done, you can wash the cooking grid with soap and water. For the maintenance of the grill, it is crucial to season the metal surfaces of the grill frequently.
Also, to prevent rusting, coat the grill with any oil or cooking spray, such as animal fat or any 100% vegetable oil.

➤ **What do I do when the gas side is too hot for Gas Char Grills?**
When this happens, try to turn the middle burner off and lower the other two. If this doesn't work, switch off the side burners and reduce the middle burner. If this still doesn't work, the only recommendation is to slightly open the lid to allow any additional heat to escape from the chamber.

➤ **What do I do when there is moisture in the thermometer?**
If you live in an environment with more interminable rain or high humidity, this will explain the moisture in the thermometer. To remove it, uninstall the thermostat from the grill, then heat it in an oven at about 350 degrees. Next, place it in a casserole dish with a lid and bake for 30 minutes. It should return to normal.
Note that if you do not quickly remove moisture from the thermometer, pressure can build in the glass and eventually break it.

➤ **How many briquettes are enough?**
Do not go over 15 briquettes at a time. If you cook with too much, it will get excessively hot and cause damage to the finish and warping of the grill.

➤ **How many meats can the Char-Griller grill at once?**
Depending on the size of the meat, the grill can conveniently handle three

good-sized ribeyes. However, some models can only manage a large family-sized steak.

> **What is the best type of charcoal to use for the Char-Griller?**
It is best to use lump charcoal, as it doesn't contain fillers or additives. This way, the burning is efficient, and the food tastes better.
Put about 15-20 lbs of charcoal at the center of the fire grate. Light the fire grates with the fire starters, never use lighter fluids. Ensure to leave the lid open until the coal is hot, and there is no expulsion of black smoke from the coals.

Chapter 4: Pork Recipes

Roasted Pork Belly

Whether you're a pork lover or not, you're going to have a change of heart once you get a taste of this amazing recipe.

Prep Time and **Cooking Time**: 1 hour | **Serves**: 6

Ingredients to Use:

- Salt and pepper to taste
- 4 teaspoons garlic powder
- 2 tablespoons paprika
- 2 teaspoons mustard powder
- 4-1/2 lb. pork belly

Step-by-Step Directions

1. Combine salt, pepper, garlic powder, paprika and mustard powder.
2. Score the pork belly but do not cut all the way through.
3. Sprinkle spice mixture all over the pork.
4. Preheat the Char-Griller to high. Prepare for indirect cooking.
5. Grill the pork over indirect high heat for 30 minutes.
6. Reduce heat to medium. Grill for another 15 minutes.
7. Let rest for 10 minutes and slice.

Serving Suggestion:

Serve with choice dip: mustard, hot sauce, ketchup.

Tip: You can also add chili powder to the spice mixture.

Teriyaki Pork

Sweet and savory teriyaki pork can definitely complete your lunch or dinner.

Prep Time and **Cooking Time**: 3 hours and 30 minutes |**Serves**: 4

Ingredients to Use:

- 1/2 cup soy sauce
- 3 tablespoons hoisin sauce
- 1/3 cup brown sugar
- 1/3 cup bourbon
- 2 cloves garlic, chopped
- 1 tablespoon ginger, chopped
- 2-1/2 pork belly, sliced
- 2 cups teriyaki sauce

Step-by-Step Directions

1. Mix soy sauce, hoisin sauce, brown sugar, bourbon, garlic and ginger in a bowl.
2. Brush pork belly with this mixture and cover with plastic wrap.
3. Marinate in the refrigerator for 3 hours.
4. Preheat Char-Griller to medium.
5. Prepare for direct grilling.
6. Grill the pork belly for 5 to 7 minutes per side.
7. Coat with teriyaki sauce and serve.

Serving Suggestion:

Serve with Jasmine rice and garnish with chopped scallions.

Tip:

Use reduced-sodium teriyaki sauce.

Garlic & Rosemary Pork Loin

The combination of garlic and rosemary definitely makes this pork loin extra special.

Prep Time and **Cooking Time**: 1 hour and 30 minutes | **Serves**: 6

Ingredients to Use:

- 6 garlic cloves
- 1/4 cup rosemary leaves
- 1 teaspoon lemon zest
- Salt and pepper to taste
- 3 tablespoons olive oil
- 1 pork loin roast

Step-by-Step Directions

1. Add garlic cloves, rosemary, lemon zest, salt, pepper and olive oil in a food processor.
2. Pulse until smooth.
3. Brush pork loin with half of this mixture.
4. Preheat Char-Griller to medium.
5. Prepare for direct grilling.
6. Grill the pork loin for 1 hour, turning every 10 minutes.
7. Brush with the remaining garlic sauce and serve.

Serving Suggestion:

Serve with roasted potatoes.

Tip:

You can also pre-boil the pork loin in water before grilling to reduce Cooking Time.

Mustard Pork Chops

You may not think of mustard as sauce for pork chops but once you try this recipe, you'd probably using this condiment for pork more often.

Prep Time and **Cooking Time**: 20 minutes | **Serves**: 6

Ingredients to Use:

- 6 pork chops
- Olive oil
- Salt and pepper to taste
- 1 tablespoon dried tarragon
- 4 tablespoons Dijon mustard

Step-by-Step Directions

1. Brush pork chops with olive oil and season with salt and pepper.
2. Sprinkle with tarragon.
3. Preheat Char-Griller to medium.
4. Prepare for direct grilling.
5. Grill the pork chops for 5 to 7 minutes per side, brushing with mustard.

Serving Suggestion:

Serve with fried potatoes.

Tip:

Use bone-in pork chops for this recipe.

Pork Chops with Carrots

This is a quick dish that would surely entice your whole family.

Prep Time and **Cooking Time**: 30 minutes | **Serves**: 4

Ingredients to Use:

- 4 pork chops
- Olive oil
- Salt and pepper to taste
- 2 cups carrot, grated
- 1/4 cup olive oil
- 1 teaspoon red wine vinegar

Step-by-Step Directions

1. Coat pork chops with oil and season with salt and pepper.
2. Preheat Char-Griller to medium.
3. Prepare for direct grilling.
4. Grill the pork chops for 3 to 6 minutes per side.
5. In a bowl, mix the remaining ingredients.
6. Serve the pork chops with the carrot slaw.

Serving Suggestion:

Serve with rice or salad.

Tip:

Use boneless pork chops for this recipe.

Lemon & Rosemary Pork Chops

You'll love how the citrusy flavor of lemon combines with the minty aroma of rosemary in this quick and satisfying recipe.

Prep Time and **Cooking Time**: 2 hours and 30 minutes |**Serves**: 4

Ingredients to Use:

4 pork chops

Marinade

- 1/4 cup olive oil
- 2 tablespoons fresh rosemary, chopped
- 2 tablespoons lemon juice
- 1 lemon, grated
- 1 tablespoon garlic, minced
- 1 tablespoon mustard
- Salt and pepper to taste

Butter

- 1 stick butter
- 1 tablespoon lemon zest
- 2 teaspoons fresh rosemary leaves
- 1 teaspoon mustard
- 1 teaspoon garlic, minced

Step-by-Step Directions

1. Add the pork chops to a baking pan.
2. Combine marinade ingredients in a bowl.
3. Marinate pork chops in this mixture for 2 hours.
4. In another bowl, mix the butter ingredients.
5. Place mixture on top of a wax paper sheet.
6. Roll into a log.
7. Refrigerate for 2 hours.
8. Preheat your Char-Griller to medium high heat.
9. Prepare for direct cooking.

10. Grill the pork chops for 3 to 5 minutes per side.
11. Transfer pork chops to a serving plate.
12. Slice butter logs and place on top of the pork chops.

Serving Suggestion:

Garnish with fresh rosemary sprigs.

Tip:

Use all-natural lump charcoal for this recipe.

Spiced Pork Chops

Do you love spicy pork chops? This is the ideal recipe for you to prepare.

Prep Time and **Cooking Time**: 20 minutes | **Serves**: 6

Ingredients to Use:

- Salt and pepper to taste
- 1 teaspoon onion powder
- 1 teaspoon paprika
- 1/2 teaspoon dried oregano leaves
- 1/2 teaspoon ground chipotle
- 1/4 teaspoon garlic powder
- 1/4 teaspoon ground cayenne pepper
- 2 tablespoons vegetable oil
- 1 tablespoon red wine vinegar
- 6 pork chops

Step-by-Step Directions

1. Combine salt, pepper, spices, oil and vinegar in a bowl.
2. Spread mixture on both sides of pork chop.
3. Cover with plastic wrap.
4. Refrigerate for 4 hours.
5. Preheat Char-Griller to medium.
6. Prepare for direct cooking.
7. Grill pork chops for 4 to 5 minutes per side.
8. Let rest for 5 minutes before serving.

Serving Suggestion:

Serve with carrot slaw.

Tip:

Trim fat from the pork chops before serving.

Thyme Pork Chops

Thyme adds something extra special to plain pork chops.

Prep Time and **Cooking Time**: 45 minutes | **Serves**: 4

Ingredients to Use:

- 1 lb. peaches, chopped
- 2 tablespoons lemon juice
- Salt and pepper to taste
- 4 pork chops
- Olive oil
- 1 tablespoon thyme, chopped

Step-by-Step Directions

1. Combine peaches, lemon juice, salt and pepper in a bowl. Set aside.
2. Brush pork chops with olive oil.
3. Season with salt, pepper and thyme.
4. Marinate for 30 minutes.
5. Preheat Char-Griller to medium high.
6. Prepare for direct cooking.
7. Grill pork chops for 4 to 5 minutes per side.
8. Top with peaches and serve.

Serving Suggestion:

Serve with your favorite dipping sauce.

Tip:

You can also top the pork chops with tomato salsa in place of peach slaw.

Ginger Pork Chops

Ginger doesn't only add flavor to pork but also ups its nutritional content.

Prep Time and **Cooking Time**: 2 hours and 30 minutes |**Serves**: 4

Ingredients to Use:

4 pork chops

Marinade

- 2 tablespoons olive oil
- 1/2 cup soy sauce
- 1/4 cup molasses
- 1/4 cup rice vinegar
- 3 tablespoons orange juice
- 1 teaspoon orange zest
- 3 cloves garlic, minced
- 1 tablespoon ginger, grated
- Pepper to taste

Step-by-Step Directions

1. Put all the marinade ingredients in a bowl.
2. Add the pork chops to the bowl and cover.
3. Marinate for 2 hours.
4. Preheat Char-Griller to medium.
5. Prepare for direct cooking.
6. Grill pork chops for 4 to 5 minutes per side.

Serving Suggestion:

Serve with roasted sweet potatoes.

Tip:

Use freshly squeezed orange juice.

Honey Mustard Pork Tenderloins

This mustard pork tenderloin is a definite must-try. For sure, everyone in the family will be delighted with this dish.

Prep Time and **Cooking Time**: 30 minutes | **Serves**: 6

Ingredients to Use:

- 2 pork tenderloins
- Olive oil

Rub

- 2 tablespoons thyme
- 1 tablespoon mustard seeds
- Salt and pepper to taste

Marinade

- 1 tablespoon Dijon mustard
- 1 tablespoon honey
- 2 teaspoons rice vinegar

Step-by-Step Directions

1. Add rub ingredients in a spice grinder.
2. Grind until powdery.
3. Mix marinade ingredients in a bowl.
4. Coat pork with oil and marinade.
5. Marinate for 30 minutes.
6. Preheat Char-Griller to medium.
7. Prepare for direct cooking.
8. Grill pork tenderloin for 4 to 5 minutes per side.

Serving Suggestion:

Serve with grilled pears or asparagus.

Tip:

You can add chili powder or chili flakes to the spice mixture if you want your pork spicy.

Chapter 5: Lamb Recipes

Rack of Lamb with Mustard

Here's a quick and simple way to cook rack of lamb that will surely be memorable for the whole family.

Prep Time and **Cooking Time**: 3 hours | **Serves**: 4

Ingredients to Use:

- 2 racks of lamb
- Olive oil
- 2 tablespoons mustard
- Salt and pepper to taste
- 1 teaspoon dried thyme, crushed
- 1/4 cup parsley, chopped

Step-by-Step Directions

1. Coat lamb with oil.
2. Spread both sides with mustard.
3. Sprinkle with salt, pepper and thyme.
4. Preheat Char-Griller to medium.
5. Prepare for direct cooking.
6. Grill rack of lamb for 12 to 15 minutes, turning once or twice.
7. Sprinkle with parsley.

Serving Suggestion:

Garnish with lemon slices.

Tip:

Use Italian parsley for this recipe.

Pita Sandwich with Lamb Patties

You'd feel like you've taken a vacation in the Middle East when you serve this authentic pita sandwich with lamb patties.

Prep Time and **Cooking Time**: 20 minutes | **Serves**: 4

Ingredients to Use:

- Pita breads

Patties

- 1 lb. ground lamb
- 1 yellow onion, grated
- 3 cloves garlic, minced
- 2 tablespoons thyme, chopped
- 2 tablespoons Italian parsley, chopped
- 1 teaspoon ground cumin
- Salt and pepper to taste

Sauce

- 1 cup yogurt
- 1 clove garlic, minced
- 4 teaspoons lemon juice
- 1/4 cup tahini
- Salt to taste

Step-by-Step Directions

1. Combine the patty ingredients.
2. Form patties from the mixture.
3. In a bowl, mix the sauce ingredients.
4. Preheat Char-Griller to high.
5. Prepare for direct cooking.
6. Grill lamb patties for 4 to 5 minutes per side.
7. Grill the pitas.
8. Serve the lamb patties on top of the pitas.
9. Drizzle with the sauce.

Serving Suggestion:

Serve with sliced cucumber, tomatoes and white onion.

Tip:

Serve with sliced cucumber, tomatoes and white onion.

Coriander Lamb Chops

Looking for a new dish to prepare for your family? Give this coriander lamb chops a try.

Prep Time and **Cooking Time**: 20 minutes | **Serves**: 4

Ingredients to Use:

- 8 lamb chops
- Olive oil

Dry rub

- 1 tablespoon mint leaves, minced
- Salt and pepper to taste
- 1 teaspoon ground coriander

Step-by-Step Directions

1. Preheat Char-Griller to medium low.
2. Prepare for direct cooking.
3. Mix the dry rub ingredients.
4. Coat lamb chops with oil.
5. Sprinkle both side with dry rub.
6. Grill lamb chops for 3 to 5 minutes per side.

Serving Suggestion:

Serve with vegetable salad.

Tip:

Let lamb chops sit for 30 minutes before grilling.

Chili Garlic Lamb Rib

Chili garlic add a unique flavor to lamb ribs.

Prep Time and **Cooking Time**: 30 minutes | **Serves**: 4

Ingredients to Use:

- 1 tablespoon olive oil
- 2 teaspoons chili powder
- 2 cloves garlic, minced
- 1 teaspoon paprika
- Salt and pepper to taste
- 4 lamb chops

Step-by-Step Directions

1. In a bowl, mix olive oil, chilli powder, garlic, paprika, salt and pepper.
2. Spread mixture on both sides of the lamb chops.
3. Preheat Char-Griller to high.
4. Prepare for direct cooking.
5. Grill lamb chops for 3 to 4 minutes per side.
6. Let rest for 3 minutes before serving.

Serving Suggestion:

Serve with fresh tomato salsa.

Tip:

You can also use rib eye steak for this recipe.

Moroccan Leg of Lamb

You're going to love this leg of lamb recipe that's easy to prepare even on a busy weeknight.

Prep Time and **Cooking Time**: 2 hours and 30 minutes |**Serves**: 8

Ingredients to Use:

- 1 leg of lamb, butterflied

Butter

- 1 stick butter, melted
- 2 teaspoon mint leaves, chopped
- 2 cloves garlic, minced
- 1 tablespoon parsley, chopped
- Salt and pepper to taste

Marinade

- 1/4 cup olive oil
- 4 cloves garlic, chopped
- 1/2 cup parsley, chopped
- 1/4 cup lemon juice
- 1 tablespoon paprika
- 2 teaspoons ground cardamom
- 1 teaspoon ground cumin
- 1 teaspoon ground turmeric
- 1 teaspoon ground ginger
- Salt to taste

Step-by-Step Directions

1. Mix marinade ingredients.
2. Divide into 2 bowls.
3. Pour first bowl into a baking pan.
4. Add leg of lamb to the baking pan.
5. Coat with the mixture, cover and marinate for 2 hours in the refrigerator.

6. Preheat Char-Griller to high.
7. Prepare for indirect cooking.
8. Grill lamb over direct heat for 10 to 15 minutes, turning every 5 minutes.
9. Move over to indirect heat and grill for 20 minutes more.
10. While waiting, mix butter ingredients.
11. Drizzle lamb with butter mixture before serving.

Serving Suggestion:

Garnish with lemon wedges.

Tip:

You can also use steaks for this recipe.

Lamb Burger

Lamb burger can be your go-to snack or dinner if you want something that's delicious and easy to prepare.

Prep Time and **Cooking Time**: 30 minutes | **Serves**: 4

Ingredients to Use:

- 1-1/2 lb. ground lamb
- 1 clove garlic, minced
- 2 tablespoons mint leaves, chopped
- Salt and pepper to taste
- 4 burger buns

Step-by-Step Directions

1. Combine ground lamb, garlic, mint leaves, salt and pepper.
2. Form patties from the mixture.
3. Preheat Char-Griller to medium.
4. Prepare for direct cooking.
5. Grill lamb burger 8 to 10 minutes, flipping once.
6. Serve with burger buns.

Serving Suggestion:

Serve with ketchup, mayo and mustard.

Tip:

Use whole-wheat burger buns.

Lamb with Chimichurri

You can't go wrong with this combination—lamb chops and chimichurri.

Prep Time and **Cooking Time**: 30 minutes | **Serves**: 4

Ingredients to Use:

- 2 lb. lamb chops
- Salt and pepper to taste
- Olive oil

Chimichurri

- 1 onion, chopped
- 4 garlic cloves, chopped
- 2 tablespoons jalapeño pepper, chopped
- 2 cups cilantro, chopped
- 3 tablespoons freshly squeezed lemon juice
- 3 tablespoons red wine vinegar
- 1/4 teaspoon red pepper flakes
- 2 tablespoons fresh oregano, chopped
- 3/4 cup olive oil
- Salt and pepper to taste

Step-by-Step Directions

1. Season lamb chops with salt and pepper.
2. Drizzle with oil.
3. Add chimichurri ingredients to a food processor.
4. Pulse until smooth.
5. Transfer to a bowl. Set aside.
6. Preheat Char-Griller to high.
7. Prepare for direct cooking.
8. Grill lamb for 3 to 4 minutes per side.
9. Serve lamb with chimichurri.

Serving Suggestion:

Garnish with fresh herb leaves or serve with grilled bell peppers.

Tip:

You can also make the chimichurri the day before and refrigerate.

Lamb Burger with Chili Sauce

You'll surely spice things up at home with this lamb burger with chili sauce.

Prep Time and **Cooking Time**: 30 minutes | **Serves**: 4

Ingredients to Use:

Sauce

- 2 roasted red bell peppers
- 3 roasted chili peppers
- 1 teaspoon olive oil
- 1 teaspoon ground cumin
- Salt and pepper to taste

Patties

- 1-1/2 lb. ground lamb
- 2 tablespoons cilantro, chopped
- Salt to taste
- 1 teaspoon ground cumin
- 1 teaspoon paprika
- 2 cloves garlic, minced
- 1/4 teaspoon ground cayenne pepper

Step-by-Step Directions

1. Preheat Char-Griller to medium. Prepare for direct cooking.
2. Combine sauce ingredients in a food processor.
3. Pulse until smooth. Set aside. Mix patty ingredients.
4. Form patties from the mixture. Grill lamb burger for 3 to 5 minutes. Serve with chili sauce.

Serving Suggestion: Serve on whole-wheat burger buns.

Tip: You can also drizzle with garlic mayo sauce in addition to the chili sauce.

Herbed Rack of Lamb

Everyone will be delighted once they get a taste of this delicious recipe—rack of lamb sprinkled with your favorite herbs.

Prep Time and **Cooking Time**: 30 minutes | **Serves**: 6

Ingredients to Use:

- 2 racks of lamb
- 3 tablespoons olive oil
- 2 teaspoon salt
- 2 teaspoons thyme, chopped
- 1 tablespoon rosemary leaves, chopped
- 1 teaspoon herbes de Provence
- 2 teaspoon garlic, minced

Step-by-Step Directions

1. Brush lamb with oil.
2. Drizzle with the salt, herbs and garlic.
3. Preheat Char-Griller to medium.
4. Prepare for direct cooking.
5. Grill the lamb for 15 to 20 minutes.

Serving Suggestion:

Serve with cooked white beans.

Tip:

Use lamb chops for this recipe and cook for 3 to 4 minutes per side.

Lamb Kebab

If you're a big fan of kebab, there's a good chance that you're going to love this lamb kebab recipe.

Prep Time and **Cooking Time**: 2 hours and 30 minutes |**Serves**: 8

Ingredients to Use:

- 1-1/2 lb. lamb, sliced into cubes

Marinade

- 2 tablespoons red wine vinegar
- 6 tablespoons olive oil
- 1 teaspoon garlic, minced
- 1 teaspoon dried oregano
- 1 teaspoon fresh mint leaves, chopped
- Salt and pepper to taste

Step-by-Step Directions

1. Combine marinade ingredients in a bowl.
2. Add lamb cubes.
3. Cover and marinate in the refrigerator for 2 hours.
4. Remove from marinade.
5. Thread onto skewers.
6. Preheat Char-Griller to medium.
7. Prepare for direct cooking.
8. Grill the lamb kebabs for 5 minutes per side.

Serving Suggestion:

Serve with grilled vegetables.

Tip:

You can also use beef for this recipe.

Chapter 6: Beef Recipes

Spiced Beef

Juicy and succulent beef encrusted with spices you can't get enough of.

Prep Time and **Cooking Time**: 1 hour and 10 minutes | **Serves**: 4

Ingredients to Use:

- 2 lb. beef roast
- 1 tablespoon brown sugar
- 1 tablespoon black peppercorns
- 2 tablespoons coriander seeds
- 1 tablespoon mustard powder
- 1 tablespoon paprika
- 1 tablespoon onion powder
- 1 tablespoon garlic powder
- Salt to taste

Step-by-Step Directions

1. Place beef in a baking pan.
2. In a spice grinder, add the rest of the ingredients.
3. Grind the spices. Rub the spice mixture all over the beef roast.
4. Preheat Char-Griller to medium.
5. Grill beef over direct heat for 5 to 7 minutes per side.

Serving Suggestion:

Serve with mashed potatoes.

Tip:

Internal temperature of beef should read 150 degrees F.

Korean Beef

You don't have to visit a Korean restaurant when you can prepare this recipe at home.

Prep Time and **Cooking Time**: 1 hour and 30 minutes | **Serves**: 4

Ingredients to Use:

- 30 oz. strip steaks

Marinade

- 1 tablespoon sesame oil
- 1/2 cup low-sodium soy sauce
- 1 tablespoon ginger, grated
- 2 cloves garlic, crushed and minced
- 2 tablespoons brown sugar

Sauce

- 1/4 cup Korean chilli paste
- 1 tablespoon sesame oil
- 1 tablespoon brown sugar
- 1 tablespoon soy sauce
- 1 tablespoon water
- 1 tablespoon rice vinegar
- 1 tablespoon olive oil
- 1 clove garlic, minced

Step-by-Step Directions

1. Mix all the marinade ingredients in a bowl.
2. Add the steaks to the bowl and cover.
3. Marinate for 1 hour in the refrigerator.
4. In another bowl, combine the sauce ingredients.
5. Preheat the Char-Griller to medium.
6. Grill the strip steaks over direct heat for 5 to 7 minutes per side.
7. Transfer steaks to a cutting board.
8. Let rest and slice.

Serving Suggestion:

Sprinkle with chopped scallions and serve with rice.

Tip:

You can also use other types of steak for this recipe.

Filet Mignon

You'd feel like you're in a fancy restaurant when you whip up this special dinner at home.

Prep Time and **Cooking Time**: 30 minutes | **Serves**: 4

Ingredients to Use:

- 4 tenderloin steaks
- Olive oil
- Salt and pepper to taste
- 2 oz. bacon, cooked crisp and chopped

Step-by-Step Directions

1. Coat the steaks with olive oil.
2. Sprinkle with salt and pepper.
3. Let sit for 15 minutes.
4. Preheat your Char-Griller to medium high.
5. Grill the steaks over direct heat for 4 to 5 minutes per side.
6. Let rest for 5 minutes.
7. Sprinkle with crispy bacon bits.

Serving Suggestion:

Serve with fresh green salad.

Tip:

Use thick-cut tenderloin steaks for this recipe.

Roast Beef

Roast beef is everyone's favorite. Make roast beef in a Char-Griller to make it extra special.

Prep Time and **Cooking Time**: 1 hour and 30 minutes | **Serves**: 6

Ingredients to Use:

- 4 lb. rib roast
- Olive oil

Rub

- 1 teaspoon mustard
- 1 teaspoon dried thyme
- 1 teaspoon garlic salt
- 1 teaspoon celery salt
- 1 teaspoon coriander seeds
- Black pepper to taste

Step-by-Step Directions

1. Add rub ingredients to a spice grinder.
2. Pulse to grind the spices.
3. Drizzle rib roast with oil and then sprinkle with spice mixture.
4. Let sit for 30 minutes.
5. Preheat your Char-Griller to medium high.
6. Add the beef to the grill over indirect heat.
7. Grill for 1 hour.
8. Slice thinly and serve.

Serving Suggestion:

Serve with steamed veggies or buttered corn and carrots.

Tip:

Let rest for at least 15 minutes before slicing.

Beef Brisket

Enjoy every bite of this delicious beef brisket.

Prep Time and **Cooking Time**: 8 hours | **Serves**: 10

Ingredients to Use:

- 12 lb. beef brisket (whole), fat trimmed
- 1/4 cup salt
- 1/4 cup black pepper
- 2 cups barbecue sauce

Step-by-Step Directions

1. Season beef brisket with salt and pepper.
2. Wrap with wax paper.
3. Refrigerate for 2 hours.
4. Preheat your Char-Griller to 450 degrees F.
5. Grill the brisket for 3 hours, turning once or twice.
6. Baste with half of barbecue sauce and grill for another 2 hours.
7. Place on a cutting board and let rest.
8. Slice thinly.
9. Drizzle with remaining barbecue sauce.

Serving Suggestion:

Serve with rice or burger buns.

Tip:

Slice across the grain.

Grilled Steak with Green Salsa

Juicy, delicious and refreshing—this grilled steak is surely a crowd pleaser.

Prep Time and **Cooking Time**: 1 hour | **Serves**: 6

Ingredients to Use:

Steak marinade

- 2 tablespoons olive oil
- 1 clove garlic, crushed
- 1 teaspoon ground cumin
- 1 teaspoon paprika
- Salt and pepper to taste
- 2 lb. skirt steak

Salsa

- 2 cups scallions, chopped
- 1 cup cilantro, chopped
- 1 jalapeño pepper, chopped
- 2 tablespoons capers, drained
- 2 tablespoons lime juice
- 1 tablespoon red wine vinegar
- 1/2 teaspoon sugar
- 1/4 teaspoon black pepper

Step-by-Step Directions

1. Combine steak marinade ingredients except skirt steak in a bowl.
2. Mix well.
3. Add skirt steak to the mixture.
4. Cover and marinate for 30 minutes.
5. Prepare Char-Griller for direct cooking.
6. Preheat to 350 degrees F.
7. Grill steak for 3 to 5 minutes per side.
8. In another bowl, mix the salsa ingredients.
9. Top the steak with the green salsa.

Serving Suggestion:

Serve with grilled corn.

Tip:

Use freshly squeezed lemon juice.

Rib Eye Steak

You can't go wrong with a recipe as simple as this. The results are absolutely spectacular.

Prep Time and **Cooking Time**: 40 minutes | **Serves**: 4

Ingredients to Use:

- 4 rib eye steaks
- 1-1/2 tablespoons olive oil
- Salt and pepper to taste

Step-by-Step Directions

1. Preheat Char-Griller to 300 degrees F.
2. Rub both sides of oil with oil.
3. Sprinkle with salt and pepper.
4. Grill the steaks for 10 minutes per side.
5. Transfer steaks to a plate.
6. Increase heat to 450 degrees F.
7. Put the steaks back to the grill.
8. Cook for 2 to 3 minutes per side.

Serving Suggestion:

Serve with fresh green salad.

Tip:

Choose steaks that are about 1-1/2 inch thick.

Steak & Potatoes

A classic combination that will definitely become a part of your weekly menu.

Prep Time and **Cooking Time**: 40 minutes | **Serves**: 5

Ingredients to Use:

- 4 rib eye steaks
- Olive oil
- 4 tablespoons steak seasoning
- 2 lb. potatoes, roasted

Step-by-Step Directions

1. Prepare Char-Griller for direct grilling over medium heat.
2. Brush steaks with oil and sprinkle with steak seasoning.
3. Grill the steaks for 3 to 5 minutes per side.
4. Serve with the roasted potatoes.

Serving Suggestion:

Serve with grilled corn or asparagus.

Tip:

Sprinkle roasted potatoes with dried basil or Parmesan cheese.

Beer Skewered Steaks

This isn't your usual way of cooking steaks but for sure, you'd have fun with this recipe.

Prep Time and **Cooking Time**: 5 hours | **Serves**: 4

Ingredients to Use:

- 1-1/2 lb. skirt steak, sliced into smaller pieces

Marinade

- 2 tablespoons freshly squeezed lime juice
- 1/2 cup beer
- 1 tablespoon chili-garlic sauce
- 2 tablespoons brown sugar
- 1 tablespoon vegetable oil
- 1 tablespoon Dijon mustard
- 2 cloves garlic, minced
- 2 teaspoons ground cumin
- Salt to taste

Step-by-Step Directions

1. Mix marinade ingredients in a bowl. Add the steak and cover.
2. Marinate in the refrigerator for 4 hours.
3. Preheat Char-Griller to medium.
4. Prepare it for direct grilling.
5. Thread the beef onto the skewers.
6. Grill for 3 to 6 minutes per side.

Serving Suggestion:

Serve with hot sauce.

Tip:

Use dark beer for this recipe.

Steak with Garlic Butter

Garlic butter definitely ups the ante of any steak dish.

Prep Time and **Cooking Time**: 1 hour and 50 minutes | **Serves**: 4

Ingredients to Use:

Garlic Butter

- 2 teaspoon cloves garlic, minced
- 1 stick butter
- 1 teaspoon lemon zest
- 1/4 cup parsley, chopped

Steaks

- 4 steaks
- Olive oil
- Salt and pepper to taste

Step-by-Step Directions

1. Mix the garlic butter ingredients in a bowl.
2. Spread this on top of a small plastic wrap.
3. Roll into a log. Refrigerate this for 1 hour.
4. Preheat Char-Griller to medium. Prepare it for direct grilling.
5. Brush steaks with oil and sprinkle with salt and pepper.
6. Grill for 3 to 5 minutes per side.
7. Transfer to a plate.
8. Add the garlic butter log on top and let it melt before serving.

Serving Suggestion:

Serve with green salad or mashed potatoes.

Tip:

You can also make the garlic butter log the day before.

Chapter 7: Chicken & Poultry Recipes

Roast Chicken with Potatoes

Roast chicken is a classic dish in gatherings but you don't have to wait for a special occasion to enjoy this dish.

Prep Time and **Cooking Time**: 1 hour and 50 minutes | **Serves**: 4

Ingredients to Use:

- 4 potatoes, sliced into wedges
- 4 tablespoons olive oil
- 1 sprig parsley
- 1 sprig thyme
- 1 sprig rosemary
- Salt to taste
- 1 whole chicken

Step-by-Step Directions

1. Fill a pot with water.
2. Add some salt.
3. Add the potatoes.
4. Bring to a boil.
5. Cook for 10 minutes.
6. Drain and let cool.
7. Toss in a little oil and salt.
8. Chop the herbs.
9. Rub chicken with remaining oil and salt.
10. Sprinkle all sides with herbs.
11. Place chicken on a roaster.
12. Preheat Char-Griller to medium.
13. Prepare for direct cooking.
14. Add the potatoes to the grill.
15. Grill for 10 minutes.

16. Transfer to a plate.
17. Add the chicken and grill for 1 hour and 20 minutes.
18. Serve chicken with potatoes.

Serving Suggestion:

Garnish with herb sprigs.

Tip:

Internal temperature of chicken should be 165 degrees F.

Barbecue Chicken

Sweet savory chicken drumsticks—you can make this easily at home when you follow this simple recipe.

Prep Time and **Cooking Time**: 1 hour and 30 minutes | **Serves**: 8

Ingredients to Use:

Dry rub

- 1-1/2 teaspoons granulated onion
- 1-1/2 teaspoons granulated garlic
- 1 tablespoon brown sugar
- 2 tablespoons paprika
- 1 teaspoon chili powder
- 1 teaspoon dried oregano
- Salt and pepper to taste

Chicken and sauce

- 16 to 18 chicken drumsticks
- 1 cup barbecue sauce

Step-by-Step Directions

1. Mix dry rub ingredients in a bowl. Coat drumsticks with the dry rub. Preheat Char-Griller to medium low.
2. Prepare for indirect cooking. Grill chicken for 15 minutes.
3. Brush with the barbecue sauce.
4. Flip and brush with the sauce three times more.
5. Cook for a total of 1 hour.

Serving Suggestion:

Serve with hot sauce.

Tip:

If possible, use sweet paprika for this recipe.

Roast Turkey

Here's another classic dish that everyone at home will rave about—roast turkey.

Prep Time and **Cooking Time**: 1 hour and 30 minutes | **Serves**: 4

Ingredients to Use:

- 1 whole turkey, prepared
- Olive oil
- Salt and pepper to taste
- 1 lemon, sliced into wedges

Step-by-Step Directions

1. Preheat Char-Griller to medium.
2. Prepare for direct grilling.
3. Coat turkey with oil.
4. Season with salt and pepper.
5. Stuff turkey cavity with lemon wedges.
6. Add turkey to the grill.
7. Roast for 1 hour.
8. Let rest for 10 minutes before serving.

Serving Suggestion:

Serve with green salad.

Tip:

Internal temperature of turkey should be 165 degrees F.

Jerk Chicken

If you want to try something different with chicken, here's an idea you'll surely love.

Prep Time and **Cooking Time**: 1 day and 30 minutes | **Serves**: 6

Ingredients to Use:

Marinade

- 2 tablespoons olive oil
- 2 tablespoons freshly squeezed lime juice
- 2 tablespoons soy sauce
- 1/4 cup white wine vinegar
- 2 teaspoons sugar
- 1 onion, chopped
- 1 chili pepper, chopped
- 2 teaspoons ground allspice
- 4 teaspoons garlic powder
- 1 teaspoon cayenne pepper
- 2 teaspoons dried thyme
- 1 teaspoon dried sage
- 1/2 teaspoon ground cinnamon
- 1/2 teaspoon ground nutmeg
- Salt and pepper to taste

Chicken

- 12 chicken thighs

Step-by-Step Directions

1. Add all marinade ingredients in a bowl.
2. Mix well.
3. Add chicken and cover.
4. Marinate in the refrigerator for 1 day.
5. The next day, preheat Char-Griller to medium.
6. Prepare for direct grilling.

7. Grill chicken for 7 to 8 minutes per side.
8. Let rest for 3 minutes before serving.

Serving Suggestion:

Serve with sour cream.

Tip:

You can also use chicken drumsticks for this recipe.

Harissa Chicken

This chicken recipe is so full of flavor, it's definitely worth a try.

Prep Time and **Cooking Time**: 1 hour and 20 minutes | **Serves**: 4

Ingredients to Use:

- 8 chicken thighs

Marinade

- 2 red bell peppers, roasted
- 3 cloves garlic, roasted
- 1/2 cup olive oil
- 1 tablespoon red chili sauce
- 1 tablespoon lemon juice
- 1 teaspoon ginger, grated
- Salt and pepper to taste
- 1 teaspoon ground cinnamon

Step-by-Step Directions

1. Combine marinade ingredients in a food processor.
2. Pulse until smooth.
3. Transfer to a bowl.
4. Add chicken.
5. Marinate for 1 hour.
6. Preheat Char-Griller to medium.
7. Prepare for direct grilling.
8. Grill chicken for 30 minutes, flipping every 10 minutes.

Serving Suggestion:

Garnish with lemon wedges.

Tip:

Use freshly squeezed lemon juice.

Turkey with Green Salsa

Here's something that's light yet filling and full of flavor—turkey breast fillets topped with green salsa made with herbs.

Prep Time and **Cooking Time**: 3 hours | **Serves**: 4

Ingredients to Use:

Salsa

- 1/2 cup olive oil
- 1 tablespoon lemon juice
- 1 tablespoon red wine vinegar
- 2 cloves garlic
- 1 cup parsley
- 1/2 cup mint leaves
- 1/2 cup cilantro
- 1 jalapeño pepper
- 1 teaspoon lemon zest
- Salt to taste

Turkey

- 4 turkey breast fillets

Step-by-Step Directions

1. Add all salsa ingredients to the food processor.
2. Pulse until smooth.
3. Divide salsa into two bowls.
4. Add turkey fillets to the first bowl.
5. Coat evenly with the salsa.
6. Cover and marinate for 2 hours.
7. Preheat Char-Griller to medium.
8. Prepare for direct grilling.
9. Grill turkey for 3 to 5 minutes per side.
10. Spread salsa on top before serving.

Serving Suggestion:

Garnish with lemon slices.

Tip:

Score turkey breast fillet before marinating.

Lemon Butter Chicken

You can't go wrong with the combination of lemon and butter.

Prep Time and **Cooking Time**: 50 minutes | **Serves**: 4

Ingredients to Use:

Chicken

- 4 chicken breast fillets
- Salt and pepper to taste

Lemon Butter

- 1 stick butter
- 3 tablespoons parsley, chopped
- 2 teaspoons lemon zest
- 2 tablespoons lemon juice
- 3 cloves garlic, minced
- Salt and pepper to taste

Step-by-Step Directions

1. Season chicken breast fillet with salt and pepper.
2. Preheat Char-Griller to medium.
3. Prepare for direct grilling.
4. Grill chicken breast for 3 to 5 minutes per side.
5. Move over to indirect heat and grill for another 15 minutes, turning once or twice.
6. Transfer to a plate.
7. Add butter to a pan over medium low heat.
8. Let it melt.
9. Stir in the rest of the lemon butter ingredients.
10. Pour lemon butter sauce over the chicken and serve.

Serving Suggestion:

Garnish with fresh herb sprigs.

Tip:

You can also use chicken breast and slice the meat yourself and use this as fillet.

Rosemary & Lemon Chicken

Lemon goes well with many herbs. One of the best herbs to pair with lemon is rosemary, as you'll see in this recipe.

Prep Time and **Cooking Time**: 2 hours and 30 minutes |**Serves**: 4

Ingredients to Use:

Marinade

- 5 tablespoons olive oil
- 2 cloves garlic, minced
- 1 tablespoon lemon juice
- 1 tablespoon rosemary leaves, chopped
- Salt and pepper to taste

Chicken

- 4 chicken breast fillet

Step-by-Step Directions

1. Add all marinade ingredients in a bowl. Mix well.
2. Add the chicken and coat evenly with marinade.
3. Cover and refrigerate for 2 hours.
4. Preheat Char-Griller to medium.
5. Prepare for direct grilling.
6. Grill chicken for 4 to 5 minutes per side.

Serving Suggestion:

Garnish with lemon slices and herb sprigs.

Tip:

Trim fat from the chicken before marinating.

Chicken Kebab

Chicken kebab is always a big hit during parties, but you can enjoy this amazing chicken recipe anytime at home.

Prep Time and **Cooking Time**: 1 hour and 30 minutes | **Serves**: 4

Ingredients to Use:

Marinade

- 2 cloves garlic, minced
- 1/4 cup olive oil
- 2 tablespoons lemon juice
- 1/4 cup yogurt
- 1 tablespoon harissa
- 1 tablespoon fresh oregano, chopped
- Salt to taste

Chicken

- 4 chicken breast fillets, sliced into smaller pieces

Step-by-Step Directions

1. Mix all marinade ingredients in a bowl.
2. Coat chicken with marinade. Cover and refrigerate for 1 hour.
3. Preheat Char-Griller to medium.
4. Prepare for direct grilling.
5. Thread chicken pieces onto metal or bamboo skewers.
6. Grill over direct heat for 4 to 5 minutes per side.

Serving Suggestion:

Serve with salad or brown rice.

Tip:

Let chicken come to room temperature for 20 minutes before grilling.

Pineapple Chicken Breast

Get the taste of the tropics in this simple but spectacular pineapple chicken recipe.

Prep Time and **Cooking Time**: 30 minutes | **Serves**: 4

Ingredients to Use:

Glaze

- 1 bell pepper, chopped
- 1 cup pineapple pre**Serves**
- 1 cup fresh pineapple, chopped
- 1/2 teaspoon red pepper flakes
- 4 teaspoons lemon juice
- 1 tablespoon lemon zest
- Salt to taste

Chicken

- 4 chicken breast fillets
- 1 tablespoon olive oil
- Salt and pepper to taste

Step-by-Step Directions

1. Add glaze ingredients to a pan over medium heat.
2. Cook for 5 minutes, stirring frequently.
3. Transfer to a bowl and set aside.
4. Preheat Char-Griller to medium.
5. Prepare for direct grilling.
6. Coat chicken breast with oil and season with salt and pepper.
7. Grill chicken for 5 to 7 minutes per side.
8. Brush with the glaze.
9. Pour the remaining glaze on top of the chicken and serve.

Serving Suggestion:

Serve with hot Jasmine rice.

Tip:

You can also use turkey fillet for this recipe.

Chapter 8: Vegan & Vegetarian Recipes

Portobello Mushrooms with Feta & Greens

You don't have to be a vegetarian to enjoy this amazing dish!

Prep Time and **Cooking Time**: 30 minutes | **Serves**: 4

Ingredients to Use:

- 4 Portobello mushrooms, gilled removed
- 1 tablespoons olive oil
- 2 cups Swiss chard, chopped and steamed
- 1/4 cup Parmesan cheese
- 2 scallions, chopped
- 1 clove garlic, minced
- 1/4 cup breadcrumbs
- 1/2 cup feta cheese, crumbled
- 1/2 cup mozzarella cheese

Step-by-Step Directions

1. Preheat Char-Griller to high.
2. Prepare for direct grilling.
3. Place Portobello mushrooms in a baking pan.
4. Mix the remaining ingredients except feta and mozzarella cheese in a bowl.
5. Stuff mushrooms with the mixture.
6. Top with the cheeses.
7. Place on top of the grill.
8. Grill for 8 to 10 minutes.

Serving Suggestion:

Serve as side dish or appetizer.

Tip:

You can also use other types of mushroom for this recipe.

Grilled Zucchini with Pesto

This is one vegetarian dish that you'd surely want to prepare over and over.

Prep Time and **Cooking Time**: 20 minutes | **Serves**: 4

Ingredients to Use:

Pesto

- 1 cup basil leaves
- 2 cloves garlic
- 1 tablespoon pine nuts
- Salt to taste
- 1 cup olive oil
- 1/4 cup Parmesan cheese

Zucchini

- 2 zucchinis, sliced in half lengthwise
- 1 tablespoon olive oil
- Pepper to taste

Step-by-Step Directions

1. Add pesto ingredients to a food processor. ulse until smooth.
2. Transfer to a bowl and set aside.
3. Preheat Char-Griller to high.
4. Prepare for direct grilling.
5. Brush zucchini with oil and season with pepper.
6. Grill for 2 to 3 minutes per side.
7. Spread pesto on top of the zucchini and serve.

Serving Suggestion:

Serve with additional pesto sauce.

Tip:

You can also use summer squash for this recipe.

Brussels Sprouts with Onion & Bacon

Here's a simple but satisfying vegetable dish you and your family will love.

Prep Time and **Cooking Time**: 30 minutes | **Serves**: 4

Ingredients to Use:

- 1 onion, sliced
- 1 lb. Brussels sprouts
- 6 cloves garlic, sliced
- Salt and pepper to taste
- 2 teaspoons red wine vinegar
- 4 bacon, cooked crisp and chopped

Step-by-Step Directions

1. Preheat Char-Griller to medium.
2. Prepare for direct grilling.
3. Place a griddle on top of the grill.
4. Add the onion and garlic.
5. Cook for 3 minutes.
6. Stir in the rest of the ingredients.
7. Cook for another 8 minutes.

Serving Suggestion:

Serve with main course.

Tip:

Remove bacon to turn this into a vegan recipe.

Butternut Squash with Sweetened Pecans

This is the vegetable dish for the sweet tooth. For sure, you'll enjoy this.

Prep Time and **Cooking Time**: 50 minutes | **Serves**: 4

Ingredients to Use:

- 1 butternut squash, sliced
- 1 stick butter, melted
- 3/4 teaspoon ground cinnamon
- Salt and pepper to taste
- 1 cup candied pecans

Step-by-Step Directions

1. Preheat Char-Griller to medium.
2. Prepare for indirect grilling.
3. Brush squash with butter.
4. Sprinkle with cinnamon, salt and pepper.
5. Grill for 1 hour.
6. Top with the candied pecans.

Serving Suggestion:

Serve with maple syrup.

Tip:

You can also use sweetened walnuts for this recipe.

Garlic Veggies

The addition of rosemary to this recipe adds something extra special to your vegetables.

Prep Time and **Cooking Time**: 30 minutes | **Serves**: 8

Ingredients to Use:

- 1 sweet potato, cubed
- 4 parsnips, cubed
- 4 carrots, cubed
- 3 tablespoons olive oil
- 2 teaspoons garlic, minced
- 2 tablespoons fresh rosemary, chopped
- Salt and pepper to taste

Step-by-Step Directions

1. Boil vegetables in a pot of water for 10 minutes.
2. Transfer to a grill pan.
3. Preheat Char-Griller to medium.
4. Prepare for direct grilling.
5. In a bowl, mix remaining ingredients.
6. Coat veggies with the mixture.
7. Grill the veggies for 10 minutes.

Serving Suggestion:

Garnish with fresh rosemary sprigs.

Tip:

You can also add other root veggies to this recipe like potatoes.

Eggplant Parmigiana

You don't have to visit a fancy restaurant to enjoy eggplant Parmigiana, you can now enjoy this at home.

Prep Time and **Cooking Time**: 30 minutes | **Serves**: 4

Ingredients to Use:

- 8 tomatoes, sliced in half
- 2 onion, sliced
- 1 cup olive oil
- 1 tablespoon oregano leaves
- 1/2 cup fresh basil leaves
- Salt and pepper to taste
- 4 eggplants, sliced in half lengthwise
- 1 tablespoon olive oil
- 1/4 cup Parmigiano cheese

Step-by-Step Directions

1. Preheat Char-Griller to medium.
2. Prepare for direct grilling.
3. Brush onions and tomatoes with oil.
4. Grill for 10 minutes, turning once or twice.
5. Add these to a food processor along with 1 cup olive oil, oregano, basil, salt and pepper.
6. Pour mixture into a pot over medium heat and simmer for 10 minutes.Brush eggplant with oil.
7. Grill for 3 to 5 minutes per side.
8. Top with the tomato mixture and cheese.

Serving Suggestion:

Serve with toasted bread.

Tip:

You can also use zucchini for this recipe.

Grilled Sweet Potato Salad

This is a twist to your favorite potato salad.

Prep Time and **Cooking Time**: 30 minutes | **Serves**: 8

Ingredients to Use:

- 3 sweet potatoes, sliced into cubes
- 2 tablespoons olive oil
- Salt and pepper to taste
- 1/4 cup mayonnaise
- 1/2 cup Greek yogurt
- 2 tablespoons cider vinegar
- 2 teaspoons Dijon mustard
- 2 tablespoon chives, chopped

Step-by-Step Directions

1. Preheat Char-Griller to medium low.
2. Prepare for direct grilling.
3. Preheat grill pan for 10 minutes.
4. Add sweet potatoes to grill pan.
5. Grill for 20 minutes, stirring once or twice.
6. In a bowl, mix remaining ingredients.
7. Toss sweet potatoes in this mixture.

Serving Suggestion:

Serve chilled.

Tip:

Use low-fat yogurt and light mayonnaise for this recipe.

Grilled Corn with Butter & Parmesan Cheese

This is a filling snack that's simple and easy to prepare.

Prep Time and **Cooking Time**: 20 minutes | **Serves**: 4

Ingredients to Use:

Butter

- 1/4 cup butter
- 1/4 teaspoon granulated garlic
- 2 tablespoons basil leaves, chopped
- 1/4 cup Parmesan cheese, grated
- Salt and pepper to taste

Corn

- 4 ears corn, husk removed

Step-by-Step Directions

1. Preheat Char-Griller to medium low.
2. Prepare for direct grilling.
3. In a bowl, combine the butter ingredients.
4. Brush a little bit of this mixture on all sides of corn.
5. Grill corn for 15 minutes, turning from time to time.
6. Spread remaining butter mixture and serve.

Serving Suggestion:

Sprinkle with fresh herbs before serving.

Tip:

Melt butter first in microwave or pan before mixing.

Grilled Asparagus

This is one of those dishes that is so simple and yet so delicious, you can't get enough of it.

Prep Time and **Cooking Time**: 15 minutes | **Serves**: 4

Ingredients to Use:

- 1/2 teaspoon garlic, minced
- 1 onion, sliced thinly
- 1 teaspoon fresh thyme, chopped
- 1 tablespoon sherry vinegar
- Salt and pepper to taste
- 4 slices bacon, cooked crisp and chopped
- 1 lb. asparagus

Step-by-Step Directions

1. Preheat Char-Griller to medium low.
2. Prepare for direct grilling.
3. In a pan over medium heat, cook onion and garlic for 1 minute.
4. Add thyme, vinegar, salt, pepper and bacon.
5. Grill asparagus for 8 minutes, turning once or twice.

Serving Suggestion:

Serve with main course.

Tip:

Remove bacon to make this recipe vegan.

Mashed Potato

Here's a unique way of preparing your favorite mashed potatoes.

Prep Time and **Cooking Time**: 30 minutes | **Serves**: 4

Ingredients to Use:

- 4 lb. potatoes, peeled
- 1 teaspoon olive oil
- Salt and pepper to taste
- 1 cup butter

Step-by-Step Directions

1. Preheat Char-Griller to medium low.
2. Prepare for indirect grilling.
3. Pierce potatoes with fork.
4. Grill potatoes for 1 hour, turning four to five times.
5. Transfer to a plate.
6. Let cool.
7. Slice and mash with a fork.
8. Stir in oil, butter, salt and pepper.

Serving Suggestion:

Sprinkle chopped fresh herbs before serving.

Tip:

You can grill for more than 1 hour until potatoes are tender.

Chapter 9: Savory Game Recipes

Lemon Deer Steak

Once you get a taste of this delicious dish, you'll never look at deer meat the same way again.

Prep Time and **Cooking Time**: 1 hour and 10 minutes | **Serves**: 4

Ingredients to Use:

- 3 tablespoons olive oil, divided
- 2 teaspoons garlic, minced
- 2 tablespoons parsley, chopped
- 2 teaspoons lemon juice
- 2 teaspoons lemon zest
- 1/4 teaspoon cayenne pepper
- Salt to taste
- 4 deer steaks

Step-by-Step Directions

1. Add all ingredients except deer steaks.
2. Marinate deer steaks in the mixture for 1 hour.
3. Preheat Char-Griller to medium.
4. Prepare for direct grilling.
5. Grill steaks for 4 to 5 minutes per side.

Serving Suggestion:

Serve with grilled asparagus.

Elk Steak with Creamy Dip

Prep Time and **Cooking Time**: 20 minutes | **Serves**: 4

Ingredients to Use:

Sauce

- 3/4 cup sour cream
- 2 tablespoons horseradish
- 2 tablespoons parsley, chopped
- 2 teaspoons Dijon mustard
- 2 teaspoons Worcestershire sauce
- Salt and pepper to taste

Steak

- 4 elk steaks
- 2 tablespoons olive oil
- Salt and pepper to taste

Step-by-Step Directions

1. Preheat Char-Griller to high.
2. Prepare for direct grilling.
3. Mix all sauce ingredients in a bowl.
4. Chill in the refrigerator until ready to serve.
5. Coat steaks with oil.
6. Season with salt and pepper.
7. Grill over high heat for 2 to 3 minutes per side.
8. Reduce heat to medium low.
9. Grill for another 5 to 8 minutes per side.

Serving Suggestion:

Serve with green salad.

Tip:

Let steak come to room temperature for 5 minutes before grilling.

Rosemary Elk Steak

Savory and succulent elk steak topped with butter flavoured with lemon juice and herbs.

Prep Time and **Cooking Time**: 2 hours and 30 minutes |**Serves**: 4

Ingredients to Use:

Marinade

- 1/2 cup olive oil
- 2 teaspoons mustard
- 1 tablespoon garlic, minced
- 3 tablespoons rosemary, chopped
- Salt and pepper to taste

Steak

- 4 elk steaks

Butter

- 1 stick butter
- 1 tablespoon lemon zest
- 4 teaspoons lemon juice
- Salt and pepper to taste
- 1 tablespoon parsley, chopped

Step-by-Step Directions

1. Combine marinade ingredients in a bowl.
2. Soak elk steaks in the marinade.
3. Cover and refrigerate for 2 hours.
4. Preheat Char-Griller to high.
5. Prepare for direct grilling.
6. Grill steaks for 4 to 6 minutes per side.
7. Mix butter ingredients in a bowl.
8. Pour into a small muffin cup.
9. Refrigerate for 15 minutes.

10. Add butter cup on top of the steak and serve.

Serving Suggestion:

Serve with mashed potatoes or roasted veggies.

Tip:

Let the steaks come to room temperature for 15 minutes before grilling.

Bison Burger

This may not be the burger on your mind, but once you get a taste of this, you'll feel you should have known about this sooner.

Prep Time and **Cooking Time**: 30 minutes | **Serves**: 4

Ingredients to Use:

- 1-1/2 lb. ground bison meat
- 1 teaspoon garlic, minced
- Salt and pepper to taste
- 1 red onion, sliced into rings
- 4 burger buns
- 4 slices bacon, cooked crisp
- Lettuce leaves
- Blue cheese

Step-by-Step Directions

1. Preheat Char-Griller to medium high.
2. Prepare for direct grilling.
3. Combine meat, garlic, salt and pepper in a bowl. ix well.
4. Form patties from the mixture.
5. Grill the patties for 4 to 5 minutes per side.
6. Toast the buns on the grill for 30 seconds.
7. Grill the onion slices for 2 minutes.
8. Assemble the burgers by adding the lettuce leaves and blue cheese on the bottom burger buns.
9. Top with the burger patty, bacon slices and onion rings.
10. Add the top of the buns.

Serving Suggestion:

Serve with ketchup and hot sauce.

Tip:

You can also use other types of game meat for this recipe.

Buffalo Steak with Chimichurri

Buffalo steak is made even more delicious by chimichurri.

Prep Time and **Cooking Time**: 50 minutes | **Serves**: 6

Ingredients to Use:

Steaks

- 2 tablespoons olive oil
- Salt and pepper to taste
- 2 teaspoons chili powder
- 2 teaspoons granulated garlic
- 1 teaspoon granulated onion
- 1/2 teaspoon dried oregano
- 1/2 teaspoon dried thyme
- 6 Buffalo steaks

Chimichurri

- 1/2 cup parsley, chopped
- 2 cloves garlic, minced
- 1/2 cup olive oil
- 2 tablespoons white wine vinegar
- 1 tablespoon water
- Salt and pepper to taste
- 1/4 teaspoon red pepper flakes

Step-by-Step Directions

1. Combine steak ingredients in a bowl except the steaks.
2. Mix well.
3. Pour into a plate.
4. Add steaks and coat with mixture.
5. Marinate for 30 minutes.
6. Preheat Char-Griller to high.
7. Prepare for indirect grilling.
8. Add chimichurri ingredients to a food processor.

9. Pulse until smooth.
10. Transfer to a bowl and set aside.
11. Grill steaks for 5 to 7 minutes per side.
12. Spread chimichurri on top and serve.

Serving Suggestion:

Serve with fresh green salad.

Tip:

You can also marinate for 4 hours or more in the refrigerator.

Bison with Spicy Sauce

Get a taste of this incredible dish when you make this recipe that's simple and easy to prepare.

Prep Time and **Cooking Time**: 50 minutes | **Serves**: 4

Ingredients to Use:

- 4 chili peppers, roasted
- 2 tablespoons olive oil

Salad

- 8 radish, sliced thinly
- 2 heads Romaine lettuce, sliced
- 1 onion, sliced
- 1 cup cilantro, sliced
- 1 cup feta cheese, crumbled

Dressing

- 6 tablespoons sour cream
- 2 tablespoons olive oil
- Pepper to taste

Steak

- 2 lb. bison steak
- 1 teaspoon ground cumin
- Salt and pepper to taste

Step-by-Step Directions

1. Add chili peppers and olive oil to a food processor.
2. Pulse until smooth.
3. Pour into a bowl and set aside.
4. Arrange salad ingredients in a serving bowl.
5. Cover and refrigerate until ready to serve.
6. Mix dressing ingredients and set aside.

7. Season steaks with cumin, salt and pepper.
8. Preheat Char-Griller to high.
9. Prepare for direct grilling.
10. Grill steaks for 5 to 6 minutes per side.
11. Serve steaks drizzled with the chili sauce, and with the salad and dressing on the side.

Serving Suggestion:

You can also serve chili sauce on the side.

Tip:

You can also use other types of game meat for this recipe.

Garlic Elk Steak

Aside from garlic, mustard is also used to flavor up elk steak in this amazingly simple recipe.

Prep Time and **Cooking Time**: 2 hours and 30 minutes | **Serves**:4

Ingredients to Use:

Paste

- 3 tablespoons olive oil
- 1 cup thyme sprigs, chopped
- 1 tablespoon garlic, minced
- 1/2 teaspoon celery seed
- 1 tablespoon balsamic vinegar
- 1 tablespoon mustard
- Salt and pepper to taste

Steaks

- 4 elk steaks

Step-by-Step Directions

1. Combine paste ingredients in a food processor.
2. Pulse until smooth.
3. Brush 2 tablespoons of mixture on both sides of steak.
4. Cover with foil and marinate in the refrigerator for 2 hours.
5. Preheat Char-Griller to high.
6. Prepare for direct grilling.
7. Grill steaks for 4 to 5 minutes per side.

Serving Suggestion:

Serve with remaining paste on the side.

Tip:

Use steaks that are at least 1 inch thick.

Deer Meat with Grilled Veggies

Pair up grilled deer meat with delicious and colorful grilled vegetables.

Prep Time and **Cooking Time**: 8 hours and 20 minutes |**Serves**: 8

Ingredients to Use:

Meat and marinade

- 3 shallots, chopped
- 1/4 cup olive oil
- 1/4 cup lemon juice
- 8 cloves garlic, peeled
- 3/4 cup fresh mint leaves, sliced
- 2 teaspoons ground coriander
- 1 tablespoon paprika
- 1 teaspoon ground ginger
- 1 teaspoon ground cinnamon
- 1 teaspoon ground turmeric
- 1 teaspoon ground cardamom
- 1/2 teaspoon ground cayenne pepper
- 1/2 teaspoon ground allspice
- Salt and pepper to taste
- 5 lb. deer meat

Vegetables

- 2 red bell peppers, sliced
- 2 zucchini, sliced
- 1 sweet potato, sliced
- 1 butternut squash, sliced
- Salt and pepper to taste
- Olive oil

Step-by-Step Directions

1. Add all marinade ingredients in a food processor.
2. Pulse until pureed.

3. Coat deer meat with marinade on both sides.
4. Cover with cling wrap.
5. Refrigerate for 8 hours.
6. Preheat Char-Griller to high.
7. Prepare for direct grilling.
8. Add vegetables to a roasting pan.
9. Toss in oil, salt and pepper.
10. Grill the vegetables for 5 minutes.
11. Grill the deer meat for 10 minutes per side.
12. Serve deer with grilled veggies.

Serving Suggestion:

Serve with hot rice.

Tip:

Let meat come to room temperature for 1 hour before grilling.

Deer Steak with Blue Cheese

Yes, blue cheese has been used to make deer steak even more delectable.

Prep Time and **Cooking Time**: 30 minutes | **Serves**: 4

Ingredients to Use:

Sauce

- 1 stick butter
- 1/4 teaspoon granulated garlic
- 2 oz. blue cheese, crumbled
- Pepper to taste

Steaks

- 4 deer steaks
- Olive oil
- Salt and pepper to taste

Step-by-Step Directions

1. Mix sauce ingredients in a bowl.
2. Mash with a fork and mix well.
3. Preheat Char-Griller to high.
4. Prepare for direct grilling.
5. Coat steaks with oil and season with salt and pepper.
6. Grill steaks for 3 to 4 minutes per side.
7. Drizzle with sauce over the steaks and serve.

Serving Suggestion:

Garnish with lemon wedges.

Tip:

Let meat come to room temperature for 15 minutes before grilling.

Elk Meat with Grilled Potatoes

Make your meat dish even more delicious with the addition of grilled potatoes.

Prep Time and **Cooking Time**: 30 minutes | **Serves**: 4

Ingredients to Use:

Seasoning

- 3 cloves garlic, chopped
- 1 tablespoon rosemary, chopped
- 2 teaspoons thyme, chopped
- Salt and pepper to taste

Meat & potatoes

- Olive oil
- 8 elk steaks
- 2 lb. potatoes

Step-by-Step Directions

1. Mix seasoning ingredients in a bowl.Drizzle elk steaks and potatoes with oil. prinkle with seasoning.
2. Preheat Char-Griller to medium. repare for direct grilling.
3. Grill potatoes for 15 minutes, flipping every 5 minutes.
4. Grill meat for 4 to 5 minutes per side.
5. Serve steak with potatoes.

Serving Suggestion:

Serve with mustard and hot sauce.

Tip:

Let meat come to room temperature for 20 minutes before serving.

Chapter 10: Side Dishes

Asparagus with Egg

Simple but satisfying—this side dish made with fried egg and grilled asparagus and cherry tomatoes is definitely worth a try.

Prep Time and **Cooking Time**: 10 minutes | **Serves**: 2

Ingredients to Use:

Vinaigrette

- 4 tablespoons olive oil
- 1 tablespoon lemon juice
- 2 cups watercress
- Salt and pepper to taste

Veggies

- 8 asparagus, trimmed and sliced
- 10 cherry tomatoes, sliced
- Olive oil

Eggs

- 2 eggs, fried
- Salt and pepper

Step-by-Step Directions

1. Add vinaigrette ingredients to a food processor.
2. Pulse until smooth.
3. Preheat Char-Griller to medium.
4. Prepare for indirect grilling.
5. Grill asparagus and tomatoes using a grill pan.
6. Cook for 5 minutes.

7. Toss grilled veggies in oil.
8. Arrange veggies in a platter.
9. Drizzle with vinaigrette.
10. Top with fried eggs.
11. Sprinkle with salt and pepper.

Serving Suggestion:

Garnish with lemon wedges.

Tip:

Add more oil to the food processor if you want your vinaigrette thinner.

Grilled Onion with Sour Cream

You're going to love the fusion of flavors in this grilled onion and sour cream side dish recipe.

Prep Time and **Cooking Time**: 40 minutes | **Serves**: 4

Ingredients to Use:

Grilled onions

- 3 white onions, sliced into rings
- 2 tablespoons olive oil
- 1 teaspoon thyme, chopped
- Salt to taste

Dip

- 1 clove garlic, minced
- 4 oz. cream cheese
- 1 cup sour cream
- 1/4 cup mayonnaise
- 1 teaspoon Worcestershire sauce
- 1/4 teaspoon hot sauce
- 2 tablespoons chives, chopped
- Salt and pepper to taste

Step-by-Step Directions

1. Preheat Char-Griller to medium. repare for direct grilling.
2. Toss onions in oil and season with thyme and salt.
3. Add onions to a grill pan.
4. Grill for 30 minutes, turning every 5 minutes.
5. Add dip ingredients to a food processor.
6. Pulse until smooth. erve onions with dip.

Serving Suggestion: **Garnish with chopped chives.**

Tip: **Use light mayonnaise for this recipe.**

Grilled Artichokes with Spinach Dip

Pair grilled artichokes with this wonderful creamy spinach dip.

Prep Time and **Cooking Time**: 30 minutes | **Serves**: 4

Ingredients to Use:

- 28 oz. artichoke hearts, trimmed and prepared
- Olive oil
- Salt and pepper to taste

Dip

- 1 lb. spinach, chopped
- 1 onion, chopped
- 3 cloves garlic, chopped
- 2 shallots, chopped
- 2 cups sour cream
- 2 cups cream
- 2 tablespoons Parmesan cheese, grated

Step-by-Step Directions

1. Preheat Char-Griller to medium.
2. Prepare for indirect grilling.
3. Brush artichokes with oil and sprinkle with salt and pepper.
4. Grill for 9 minutes, turning every 3 minutes.
5. In a pan over medium heat, add some more oil.
6. Cook spinach, onion and garlic for 3 minutes.
7. Remove from heat. ransfer to a food processor.
8. Add the rest of the dip ingredients. rocess until smooth.
9. Serve artichoke with dip.

Serving Suggestion:

Serve with pita chips.

Tip:

You can also thread artichoke hearts onto skewers before grilling.

Chicken Nachos

This is not just a side dish but can also be served as snack or appetizer.

Prep Time and **Cooking Time**: 30 minutes | **Serves**: 6

Ingredients to Use:

Paste

- 2 tablespoons olive oil
- 1 teaspoon dried oregano
- 1 teaspoon onion powder
- 2 teaspoons chili powder
- 1/2 teaspoon ground cumin
- Salt to taste

Nachos

- 8 oz. chicken breast fillet
- 14 oz. tortilla chips
- 1 red bell pepper, sliced
- 5 scallions, chopped
- 1 lb. pepper Jack cheese

Step-by-Step Directions

1. Combine all paste ingredients in a bowl.
2. Coat chicken with the paste mixture. arinate for 30 minutes.
3. Preheat Char-Griller to medium. repare for indirect grilling.
4. Grill chicken for 5 to 6 minutes per side.
5. Arrange tortilla chips on a baking pan.
6. Top with grilled chicken, bell pepper, scallions and cheese.
7. Place in the grill and cook until the cheese has melted.

Serving Suggestion: **Serve with salsa and sour cream.**

Tip:

Remove chicken if you want a vegetarian side dish.

Grilled Tuna on Toasted Bread

This isn't like your regular side dish, this one is light, delicious and healthy all at the same time.

Prep Time and **Cooking Time**: 20 minutes | **Serves**: 10

Ingredients to Use:

- 2 tuna fillets
- Olive oil
- Salt and pepper to taste
- 1 teaspoon ground fennel seed

Topping

- 1/2 cup cucumber, chopped
- 1 tablespoon capers, chopped
- 2 tablespoon black olives, chopped
- 2 tablespoons fresh dill, chopped
- 1/2 cup mayonnaise
- 1 tablespoon lemon juice

Bread

- 1 baguette, sliced

Step-by-Step Directions

1. Preheat Char-Griller to medium.
2. Prepare for direct grilling.
3. Brush tuna with oil and season with salt, pepper and ground fennel.
4. Grill tuna for 4 to 5 minutes per side.
5. Transfer to a cutting board.
6. Once cool enough to handle, chop into smaller piece.
7. Add to a bowl.
8. Stir in topping ingredients.
9. Spread mixture on top of the baguette slices.

Serving Suggestion:

Serve with tomato slices and lettuce leaves.

Tip:

Each tuna fillet should be at least 8 ounces each.

Dates with Blue Cheese

This may not be the usual side dish on your mind, but for sure, you'll enjoy every bite of this dish.

Prep Time and **Cooking Time**: 30 minutes | **Serves**: 6

Ingredients to Use:

Glaze

- 1 cup balsamic vinegar
- 1/2 cup granulated sugar

Dates

- 1/2 cup pecans, chopped
- 3 oz. blue cheese
- 24 dates
- Cooking spray

Step-by-Step Directions

1. Preheat Char-Griller to medium.
2. Prepare for direct grilling.
3. Add glaze ingredients to a pan over medium heat.
4. Cook and stir until sugar has dissolved.
5. Transfer to a bowl and set aside.
6. Combine pecans and blue cheese.
7. Slice dates but not all the way through.
8. Stuff dates with blue cheese mixture.
9. Grill for 1 minute.
10. Pour glaze on top and serve.

Serving Suggestion:

Serve with shredded cabbage.

Tip:

Use soft blue cheese for this recipe.

Bruschetta with Peppers

Although this is not the bruschetta you're used to, there's a good chance that you'll love this recipe.

Prep Time and Cooking Time: 2 hours and 20 minutes | Serves:6

Ingredients to Use:

Marinated peppers

- 2 red bell peppers
- 2 tablespoons olive oil
- 2 teaspoons red wine vinegar
- 2 teaspoons rosemary, chopped
- 1 clove garlic, crushed
- Salt to taste
- Red pepper flakes
- Fresh basil leaves, chopped

Bread

- 6 slices French bread
- Olive oil
- 6 oz. Fontina cheese, grated

Step-by-Step Directions

1. Preheat Char-Griller to high. repare for direct grilling.
2. Grill peppers for 15 minutes.
3. Transfer to a cutting board and let cool.
4. Once cool, chop into strips.
5. Add the rest of the marinated peppers ingredients to a bowl.
6. Soak peppers in the mixture for 2 hours.
7. Add peppers on top of French bread slices.
8. Drizzle with oil and sprinkle with cheese.
9. Grill until the cheese has melted.

Serving Suggestion: Sprinkle with dried herbs before serving.

Tip: You can also use Italian bread for this recipe.

Cheese & Chive Bites

This is a perfect side to many types of breakfast dish.

Prep Time and **Cooking Time**: 30 minutes | **Serves**: 8

Ingredients to Use:

- 3 tablespoons butter
- 2-1/4 cups all-purpose flour
- 1-1/2 cup cheddar cheese, grated
- 3 tablespoons vegetable shortening
- 1 tablespoon granulated sugar
- 1 tablespoon baking powder
- 1 cup milk
- 1/4 cup fresh chives, minced
- Salt to taste

Step-by-Step Directions

1. Preheat Char-Griller to high.
2. Prepare for direct grilling.
3. Grease a baking pan with a little bit of butter.
4. Add the remaining butter to a food processor along with the rest of the ingredients.
5. Process until fully combined. nead mixture into a dough.
6. Flatten dough and cut biscuits from the mixture using a biscuit cutter.
7. Transfer to the baking pan. rill with the lid closed for 20 minutes.

Serving Suggestion:

Top with butter cubes and serve.

Tip:

Use whole milk for this recipe.

Mac & Cheese

This mac and cheese is made even more special with a layer of Parmesan crumbs.

Prep Time and **Cooking Time**: 30 minutes | **Serves**: 8

Ingredients to Use:

- 1-1/2 teaspoons granulated onion
- 1/4 cup butter
- 2 teaspoons mustard powder
- 1/4 cup all-purpose flour
- 2 cups Monterey Jack cheese, shredded
- 1 cup cheddar cheese, shredded
- 3-1/2 cups milk
- 1 lb. elbow macaroni, cooked according to package directions
- Salt and pepper to taste
- 1 cup panko bread crumbs
- 1 cup Parmesan cheese
- 3 tablespoons melted butter

Step-by-Step Directions

1. Preheat Char-Griller to high. repare for direct grilling.
2. In a pan over medium heat, cook onion in butter for 2 minutes.
3. Stir in mustard powder, flour, cheeses and whole milk.
4. Add macaroni to the sauce. Season with salt and pepper.
5. Transfer to a baking pan.
6. Toast breadcrumbs and Parmesan cheese in melted butter.
7. Pour on top of the pasta. rill for 25 minutes with the lid closed.

Serving Suggestion: **Garnish with chopped fresh herbs.**

Tip:

Use whole milk for this recipe.

Artichoke Dip with Parmesan Cheese

Another Parmesan cheese recipe that everyone in your family will love.

Prep Time and **Cooking Time**: 30 minutes | **Serves**: 6

Ingredients to Use:

- 14 oz. artichoke hearts
- 6 oz. cream cheese
- 1 cup mayonnaise
- 1/4 cup sour cream
- 1 cup mozzarella cheese, shredded
- 4 oz. green chili peppers
- 1 teaspoon mustard powder
- 2 teaspoons garlic, minced
- 1/4 cup Parmesan cheese
- 1/4 teaspoon hot sauce
- Salt and pepper to taste

Step-by-Step Directions

1. Preheat Char-Griller to medium high.
2. Prepare for indirect grilling.
3. Grill artichoke hearts for 5 minutes.
4. Chop artichokes.
5. Add to a bowl.
6. Stir in the rest of the ingredients.

Serving Suggestion:

Serve with baguette slices.

Tip:

Add chilli powder if you want it spicier.

Conclusion

Grilling is exciting, especially with a grill that satisfies all your demands. The Char-Griller creates magic by bringing out the best in your meat and vegetables. Enjoy this weekend and every other weekend for the next two months with meals prepared on the Char-Griller.

Good luck!

CPSIA information can be obtained
at www.ICGtesting.com
Printed in the USA
LVHW050204031222
734429LV00004B/37